JAMES SIMON

A Pocketful of Christmas Poems

Joyful Ink
Publishing's

Contents

Introduction

When winter settles in, and the world is covered in a soft layer of snow, there's a quiet magic that fills the air. The long nights, the glow of firelight, and the hush of snowfall all invite moments of pause and reflection. A Pocketful of Christmas Poems captures this atmosphere, offering a selection of poetry that speaks to the heart of the season.

Picture yourself by the fire, wrapped in a blanket, with a warm drink at your side. Outside, the snow drifts gently down, while inside, you turn the pages of this collection, discovering poems that celebrate the warmth of home, the joy of gathering, and the beauty of the winter landscape. Whether reading alone or sharing the words with loved ones, these poems create a space for connection and nostalgia, recalling simpler times and timeless traditions.

Featuring the works of Lydia Maria Child, Robert Frost, William Blake, and many more, this anthology draws on rich poetic voices to bring the season to life. Christmas is not just a time for festivities, but also a chance to reflect on the year that's passed and to enjoy time with the people who matter most. Each poem is a reminder of the moments that make this season special—a time to slow down, reflect, and appreciate the simple pleasures of the winter months.

Twas The Night Before Christmas

'Twas the night before Christmas, when all through
the house
Not a creature was stirring, not even a mouse;
The stockings were hung by the chimney with care
In hopes that St. Nicholas soon would be there;

The children were nestled all snug in their beds,
While visions of sugar-plums danced in their heads;
And mamma in her kerchief, and I in my cap,
Had just settled our brains for a long winter's nap,

When out on the lawn there arose such a clatter,
I sprang from the bed to see what was the matter.
Away to the window I flew like a flash,
Tore open the shutters and threw up the sash.

The moon on the breast of the new-fallen snow
Gave the lustre of mid-day to objects below,
When, what to my wondering eyes should appear,
But a miniature sleigh, and eight tiny reindeer,

With a little old driver, so lively and quick,
I knew in a moment it must be St. Nick.
More rapid than eagles his coursers they came,
And he whistled, and shouted, and called them by
name:

"Now, *Dasher!* now, *Dancer!* now, *Prancer* and *Vixen!*
On, *Comet!* on, *Cupid!* on, *Donder* and *Blitzen!*
To the top of the porch! to the top of the wall!
Now dash away! dash away! dash away all!"

As dry leaves that before the wild hurricane fly,
When they meet with an obstacle, mount to the sky;
So up to the house-top the coursers they flew,
With the sleigh full of Toys, and St. Nicholas too.

And then, in a twinkling, I heard on the roof
The prancing and pawing of each little hoof.
As I drew in my head, and was turning around,
Down the chimney St. Nicholas came with a bound.

He was dressed all in fur, from his head to his foot,
And his clothes were all tarnished with ashes and
soot;
A bundle of Toys he had flung on his back,
And he looked like a peddler just opening his pack.

His eyes—how they twinkled! his dimples how

merry!
His cheeks were like roses, his nose like a cherry!
His droll little mouth was drawn up like a bow,
And the beard of his chin was as white as the snow;

The stump of a pipe he held tight in his teeth,
And the smoke it encircled his head like a wreath;
He had a broad face and a little round belly,
That shook when he laughed, like a bowlful of jelly.

He was chubby and plump, a right jolly old elf,
And I laughed when I saw him, in spite of myself;
A wink of his eye and a twist of his head,
Soon gave me to know I had nothing to dread;

He spoke not a word, but went straight to his work,
And filled all the stockings; then turned with a jerk,
And laying his finger aside of his nose,
And giving a nod, up the chimney he rose;

He sprang to his sleigh, to his team gave a whistle,
And away they all flew like the down of a thistle.
But I heard him exclaim, ere he drove out of sight,
"Happy Christmas to all, and to all a good-night.

Clement Clarke Moore

Noel: Christmas Eve 1913

A frosty Christmas Eve
when the stars were shining
Fared I forth alone
where westward falls the hill,
And from many a village
in the water'd valley
Distant music reach'd me
peals of bells aringing:
The constellated sounds
ran sprinkling on earth's floor
As the dark vault above
with stars was spangled o'er.
Then sped my thoughts to keep
that first Christmas of all
When the shepherds watching
by their folds ere the dawn
Heard music in the fields
and marveling could not tell
Whether it were angels
or the bright stars singing.

Now blessed be the tow'rs
that crown England so fair
That stand up strong in prayer
unto God for our souls
Blessed be their founders
(said I) an' our country folk
Who are ringing for Christ
in the belfries to-night
With arms lifted to clutch
the rattling ropes that race
Into the dark above
and the mad romping din.

But to me heard afar
it was starry music
Angels' song, comforting
as the comfort of Christ
When he spake tenderly
to his sorrowful flock:
The old words came to me
by the riches of time
Mellow'd and transfigured
as I stood on the hill
Heark'ning in the aspect
of th' eternal silence.

Robert Bridges

A Christmas Childhood

One side of the potato-pits was white with frost -
How wonderful that was, how wonderful!
And when we put our ears to the paling-post
The music that came out was magical.

The light between the ricks of hay and straw
Was a hole in Heaven's gable. An apple tree
With its December-glinting fruit we saw -
O you, Eve, were the world that tempted me.

To eat the knowledge that grew in clay
And death the germ within it! Now and then
I can remember something of the gay
Garden that was childhood's. Again.

The tracks of cattle to a drinking-place,
A green stone lying sideways in a ditch,
Or any common sight, the transfigured face
Of a beauty that the world did not touch.

My father played the melodion
Outside at our gate;
There were stars in the morning east
And they danced to his music.

Across the wild bogs his melodion called
To Lennons and Callans.
As I pulled on my trousers in a hurry
I knew some strange thing had happened.

Outside in the cow-house my mother
Made the music of milking;
The light of her stable-lamp was a star
And the frost of Bethlehem made it twinkle.

A water-hen screeched in the bog,
Mass-going feet
Crunched the wafer-ice on the pot-holes,
Somebody wistfully twisted the bellows wheel.

My child poet picked out the letters
On the grey stone,
In silver the wonder of a Christmas townland,
The winking glitter of a frosty dawn.

Cassiopeia was over
Cassidy's hanging hill,
I looked and three whin bushes rode across

The horizon — the Three Wise Kings.

And old man passing said:
'Can't he make it talk -
The melodion.' I hid in the doorway
And tightened the belt of my box-pleated coat.

I nicked six nicks on the door-post
With my penknife's big blade -
there was a little one for cutting tobacco.
And I was six Christmases of age.

My father played the melodion,
My mother milked the cows,
And I had a prayer like a white rose pinned
On the Virgin Mary's blouse.

Patrick Kavanagh

A Visit from St. Nicholas (The Christmas Poem)

Twas the night before Christmas, when all through
the house
Not a creature was stirring, not even a mouse;
The stockings were hung by the chimney with care,
In hopes that St. Nicholas soon would be there;

The children were nestled all snug in their beds,
While visions of sugar-plums danced in their heads;
And Mama in her 'kerchief, and I in my cap,
Had just settled our brains for a long winter's nap;

When out on the lawn there arose such a clatter,
I sprang from the bed to see what was the matter.
Away to the window I flew like a flash,
Tore open the shutters and threw up the sash.

The moon on the breast of the new-fallen snow,
Gave the lustre of mid-day to objects below,

When, what to my wondering sight should appear,
But a miniature sleigh, and eight tiny rein-deer,

With a little old driver, so lively and quick,
I knew in a moment it must be St. Nick.
More rapid than eagles his coursers they came,
And he whistled, and shouted, and called them by
name;

"Now, Dasher! now, Dancer! now, Prancer and
Vixen!
On, Comet! on, Cupid! on, Donner and Blitzen!
To the top of the porch! to the top of the wall!
Now dash away! dash away! dash away all!"

As dry leaves that before the wild hurricane fly,
When they meet with an obstacle, mount to the sky;
So up to the house-top the coursers they flew,
With the sleigh full of Toys, and St. Nicholas too.

And then, in a twinkling, I heard on the roof,
The prancing and pawing of each little hoof—
As I drew in my head, and was turning around,
Down the chimney St. Nicholas came with a bound.

He was dressed all in fur, from his head to his foot,
And his clothes were all tarnished with ashes and
soot;

A bundle of Toys he had flung on his back,
And he look'd like a pedlar just opening his pack.

His eyes—how they twinkled! his dimples how
merry!
His cheeks were like roses, his nose like a cherry!
His droll little mouth was drawn up like a bow,
And the beard of his chin was as white as the snow;

The stump of a pipe he held tight in his teeth,
And the smoke it encircled his head like a wreath;
He had a broad face and a little round belly,
That shook when he laughed, like a bowlfull of jelly.

He was chubby and plump, a right jolly old elf,
And I laughed when I saw him, in spite of myself;
A wink of his eye and a twist of his head,
Soon gave me to know I had nothing to dread;

He spoke not a word, but went straight to his work,
And fill'd all the stockings; then turned with a jerk,
And laying his finger aside of his nose,
And giving a nod, up the chimney he rose;

He sprang to his sleigh, to his team gave a whistle,
And away they all flew like the down of a thistle.
But I heard him exclaim, ere he drove out of sight,
"Happy Christmas to all, and to all a good night.

Clement Clarke Moore

Contentment

"Man wants but little here below"

Little I ask; my wants are few;
I only wish a hut of stone,
(A very plain brown stone will do,)
That I may call my own; —
And close at hand is such a one,
In yonder street that fronts the sun.

Plain food is quite enough for me;
Three courses are as good as ten; —
If Nature can subsist on three,
Thank Heaven for three. Amen!
I always thought cold victual nice; —
My choice would be vanilla-ice.

I care not much for gold or land; —
Give me a mortgage here and there, —
Some good bank-stock, some note of hand,
Or trifling railroad share, —

I only ask that Fortune send
A little more than I shall spend.

Honors are silly toys, I know,
And titles are but empty names;
I would, perhaps, be Plenipo,—
But only near St. James;
I'm very sure I should not care
To fill our Gubernator's chair.

Jewels are baubles; 't is a sin
To care for such unfruitful things;—
One good-sized diamond in a pin,—
Some, not so large, in rings,—
A ruby, and a pearl, or so,
Will do for me;—I laugh at show.

My dame should dress in cheap attire;
(Good, heavy silks are never dear;)—
I own perhaps I might desire
Some shawls of true Cashmere,—
Some marrowy crapes of China silk,
Like wrinkled skins on scalded milk.

I would not have the horse I drive
So fast that folks must stop and stare;
An easy gait—two forty-five—
Suits me; I do not care;—

Perhaps, for just a single spurt,
Some seconds less would do no hurt.

Of pictures, I should like to own
Titians and Raphaels three or four, —
I love so much their style and tone,
One Turner, and no more,
(A landscape, — foreground golden dirt, —
The sunshine painted with a squirt.)

Of books but few, — some fifty score
For daily use, and bound for wear;
The rest upon an upper floor; —
Some little luxury there
Of red morocco's gilded gleam
And vellum rich as country cream.

Busts, cameos, gems, — such things as these,
Which others often show for pride,
I value for their power to please,
And selfish churls deride; —
One Stradivarius, I confess,
Two Meerschaums, I would fain possess.

Wealth's wasteful tricks I will not learn,
Nor ape the glittering upstart fool; —
Shall not carved tables serve my turn,
But all must be of buhl?

Give grasping pomp its double share,—
I ask but one recumbent chair.

Thus humble let me live and die,
Nor long for Midas' golden touch;
If Heaven more generous gifts deny,
I shall not miss them much,—
Too grateful for the blessing lent
Of simple tastes and mind content!

Oliver Wendell Holmes Sr.

Christmas Fancies

When Christmas bells are swinging above the fields
of snow,
We hear sweet voices ringing from lands of long ago.
And etched on vacant places,
Are half forgotten faces
Of friends we used to cherish, and loves we used to
know —
When Christmas bells are swinging above the fields
of snow.

Uprising from the ocean of the present surging near,
We see, with strange emotion that is not free from
fear,
That continent Elysian
Long vanished from our vision,
Youth's lovely lost Atlantis, so mourned for and so
dear,
Uprising from the ocean of the present surging near.

When gloomy gray Decembers are roused to

Christmas mirth,
The dullest life remembers there once was joy on
earth,
And draws from youth's recesses
Some memory it possesses,
And, gazing through the lens of time, exaggerates
its worth,
When gloomy gray December is roused to Christmas
mirth.

When hanging up the holly or mistletoe, I wis
Each heart recalls some folly that lit the world with
bliss.
Not all the seers and sages
With wisdom of the ages
Can give the mind such pleasure as memories of that
kiss
When hanging up the holly or mistletoe, I wis.

For life was made for loving, and love alone repays,
As passing years are proving for all of Time's sad
ways.
There lies a sting in pleasure,
And fame gives shallow measure,
And wealth is but a phantom that mocks the restless
days,
For life was made for loving, and only loving pays.

When Christmas bells are pelting the air with silver
chimes,
And silences are melting to soft, melodious rhymes,
Let Love, the world's beginning,
End fear and hate and sinning;
Let Love, the God Eternal, be worshipped in all
climes
When Christmas bells are pelting the air with silver
chimes

Ella Wheeler Wilcox

New Year Snow

The white snow falls on hill and dale,
The snow falls white by square and street,
Falls on the town, a bridal veil,
And on the fields a winding-sheet.

A winding-sheet for last year's flowers,
For last year's love, and last year's tear,
A bridal veil for the New Hours,
For the New Love and the New Year.

Soft snow, spread out his winding-sheet!
Spin fine her veil, O bridal snow!
Cover the print of her dancing feet,
And the place where he lies low.

Edith Nesbit

At the Entering of the New Year

(OLD STYLE)

Our songs went up and out the chimney,
And roused the home-gone husbandmen;
Our allemands, our heys, poussettings,
Our hands-across and back again,
Sent rhythmic throbbings through the casements
On to the white highway,
Where nighted farers paused and muttered,
"Keep it up well, do they!"

The contrabasso's measured booming
Sped at each bar to the parish bounds,
To shepherds at their midnight lambings,
To stealthy poachers on their rounds;
And everybody caught full duly
The notes of our delight,
As Time unrobed the Youth of Promise
Hailed by our sanguine sight.

23

II
(NEW STYLE)

We stand in the dusk of a pine-tree limb,
As if to give ear to the muffled peal,
Brought or withheld at the breeze's whim;
But our truest heed is to words that steal
From the mantled ghost that looms in the gray,
And seems, so far as our sense can see,
To feature bereaved Humanity,
As it sighs to the imminent year its say:—

"O stay without, O stay without,
Calm comely Youth, untasked, untired;
Though stars irradiate thee about
Thy entrance here is undesired.
Open the gate not, mystic one;
Must we avow what we would close confine?
With thee, good friend, we would have converse
none,
Albeit the fault may not be thine."

December 31. During the War.

Thomas Hardy

Christ's Nativity

Awake, glad heart! get up and sing!
It is the birth-day of thy King.
Awake! awake!
The Sun doth shake
Light from his locks, and all the way
Breathing perfumes, doth spice the day.

Awake, awake! hark how th' wood rings;
Winds whisper, and the busy springs
A concert make;
Awake! awake!
Man is their high-priest, and should rise
To offer up the sacrifice.

I would I were some bird, or star,
Flutt'ring in woods, or lifted far
Above this inn
And road of sin!
Then either star or bird should be
Shining or singing still to thee.

I would I had in my best part
Fit rooms for thee! or that my heart
Were so clean as
Thy manger was!
But I am all filth, and obscene;
Yet, if thou wilt, thou canst make clean.

Sweet Jesu! will then. Let no more
This leper haunt and soil thy door!
Cure him, ease him,
O release him!
And let once more, by mystic birth,
The Lord of life be born in earth.

Henry Vaughan

The Snow-Storm

Announced by all the trumpets of the sky,
Arrives the snow, and, driving o'er the fields,
Seems nowhere to alight: the whited air
Hides hills and woods, the river, and the heaven,
And veils the farm-house at the garden's end.
The sled and traveller stopped, the courier's feet
Delayed, all friends shut out, the housemates sit
Around the radiant fireplace, enclosed
In a tumultuous privacy of storm.

Come see the north wind's masonry.
Out of an unseen quarry evermore
Furnished with tile, the fierce artificer
Curves his white bastions with projected roof
Round every windward stake, or tree, or door.
Speeding, the myriad-handed, his wild work
So fanciful, so savage, nought cares he
For number or proportion. Mockingly,
On coop or kennel he hangs Parian wreaths;
A swan-like form invests the hidden thorn;

Fills up the farmer's lane from wall to wall,
Maugre the farmer's sighs; and, at the gate,
A tapering turret overtops the work.
And when his hours are numbered, and the world
Is all his own, retiring, as he were not,
Leaves, when the sun appears, astonished Art
To mimic in slow structures, stone by stone,
Built in an age, the mad wind's night-work,
The frolic architecture of the snow.

Ralph Waldo Emerson

Christmas Bells

I heard the bells on Christmas Day
Their old, familiar carols play,
And wild and sweet
The words repeat
Of peace on earth, good-will to men!

And thought how, as the day had come,
The belfries of all Christendom
Had rolled along
The unbroken song
Of peace on earth, good-will to men!

Till ringing, singing on its way,
The world revolved from night to day,
A voice, a chime,
A chant sublime
Of peace on earth, good-will to men!

Then from each black, accursed mouth
The cannon thundered in the South,

And with the sound
The carols drowned
Of peace on earth, good-will to men!

It was as if an earthquake rent
The hearth-stones of a continent,
And made forlorn
The households born
Of peace on earth, good-will to men!

And in despair I bowed my head;
'There is no peace on earth,' I said;
'For hate is strong,
And mocks the song
Of peace on earth, good-will to men!'

Then pealed the bells more loud and deep:
'God is not dead, nor doth He sleep;
The Wrong shall fail,
The Right prevail,
With peace on earth, good-will to men.'

Henry Wadsworth Longfellow

The Oxen

Christmas Eve, and twelve of the clock.
  "Now they are all on their knees,"
An elder said as we sat in a flock
  By the embers in hearthside ease.

We pictured the meek mild creatures where
  They dwelt in their strawy pen,
Nor did it occur to one of us there
  To doubt they were kneeling then.

So fair a fancy few would weave
  In these years! Yet, I feel,
If someone said on Christmas Eve,
  "Come; see the oxen kneel,

"In the lonely barton by yonder coomb
  Our childhood used to know,"
I should go with him in the gloom,
  Hoping it might be so.

Thomas Hardy

Christmas in the Olden Time

On Christmas-eve the bells were rung;
The damsel donned her kirtle sheen;
The hall was dressed with holly green;
Forth to the wood did merry men go,
To gather in the mistletoe.
Thus opened wide the baron's hall
To vassal, tenant, serf and all;
Power laid his rod of rule aside
And ceremony doffed his pride.
The heir, with roses in his shoes,
That night might village partner choose;
The lord, underogating, share
The vulgar game of "Post and Pair."
All hailed, with uncontrolled delight,
And general voice, the happy night
That to the cottage, as the crown,
Brought tidings of salvation down.

The fire, with well-dried logs supplied,
Went roaring up the chimney wide;

The huge hall-table's oaken face,
Scrubbed till it shone, the day to grace,
Bore then upon its massive board
No mark to part the squire and lord.
Then was brought in the lusty brawn
By old blue-coated serving man;
Then the grim boar's head frowned on high,
Crested with bays and rosemary.
Well can the green-garbed ranger tell
How, when and where the monster fell;
What dogs before his death he tore,
And all the baitings of the boar.
The wassal round, in good brown bowls,
Garnished with ribbons, blithely trowls.
There the huge sirloin reeked: hard by
Plum-porridge stood, and Christmas pye;
Nor failed old Scotland to produce,
At such high-tide, her savory goose.

Then came the merry maskers in,
And carols roared with blithesome din.
If unmelodious was the song,
It was a hearty note, and strong;
Who lists may in their murmuring see
Traces of ancient mystery;
White shirts supplied the masquerade,
And smutted cheeks the visors made;
But O, what maskers richly dight,

Can boast of bosoms half so light!
England was "merry England" when
Old Christmas brought his sports again;
'Twas Christmas broached the mightiest ale,
'Twas Christmas told the merriest tale;
A Christmas gambol oft would cheer
The poor man's heart through half the year.

Walter Scott

The Waits

At the break of Christmas Day,
Through the frosty starlight ringing,
Faint and sweet and far away,
Comes the sound of children, singing,
Chanting, singing,
"Cease to mourn,
For Christ is born,
Peace and joy to all men bringing!"

Careless that the chill winds blow,
Growing stronger, sweeter, clearer,
Noiseless footfalls in the snow,
Bring the happy voices nearer;
Hear them singing,
"Winter's drear,
But Christ is here,
Mirth and gladness with Him bringing."

"Merry Christmas!" hear them say,
As the East is growing lighter;

"May the joy of Christmas Day
Make your whole year gladder, brighter!"
Join their singing,
"To each home
Our Christ has come,
All Love's treasures with Him bringing!"

Margaret Deland

Christmastide

Love came down at Christmas,
Love all lovely, Love Divine;
Love was born at Christmas,
Star and Angels gave the sign.

Worship we the Godhead,
Love Incarnate, Love Divine;
Worship we our Jesus:
But wherewith for sacred sign?

Love shall be our token,
Love be yours and love be mine,
Love to God and all men,
Love for plea and gift and sign.

Christina Rossetti

November

Yet one smile more, departing, distant sun!
One mellow smile through the soft vapory air,
Ere, o'er the frozen earth, the loud winds run,
Or snows are sifted o'er the meadows bare.
One smile on the brown hills and naked trees,
And the dark rocks whose summer wreaths are cast,
And the blue gentian flower, that, in the breeze,
Nods lonely, of her beauteous race the last.
Yet a few sunny days, in which the bee
Shall murmur by the hedge that skirts the way,
The cricket chirp upon the russet lea,
And man delight to linger in thy ray.
Yet one rich smile, and we will try to bear
The piercing winter frost, and winds, and darkened
air.

William Cullen Bryant

Home, Sweet Home

Mid pleasures and palaces though we may roam,
Be it ever so humble, there's no place like home;
A charm from the sky seems to hallow us there,
Which, seek through the world, is ne'er met with
elsewhere.
Home, home, sweet, sweet home!
There's no place like home, oh, there's no place like
home!

An exile from home, splendor dazzles in vain;
Oh, give me my lowly thatched cottage again!
The birds singing gayly, that come at my call —
Give me them — and the peace of mind, dearer than
all!
Home, home, sweet, sweet home!
There's no place like home, oh, there's no place like
home!

I gaze on the moon as I tread the drear wild,
And feel that my mother now thinks of her child,

As she looks on that moon from our own cottage
door
Thro' the woodbine, whose fragrance shall cheer me
no more.
Home, home, sweet, sweet home!
There's no place like home, oh, there's no place like
home!

How sweet 'tis to sit 'neath a fond father's smile,
And the caress of a mother to soothe and beguile!
Let others delight mid new pleasures to roam,
But give me, oh, give me, the pleasures of home.
Home, home, sweet, sweet home!
There's no place like home, oh, there's no place like
home!

To thee I'll return, overburdened with care;
The heart's dearest solace will smile on me there;
No more from that cottage again will I roam;
Be it ever so humble, there's no place like home.
Home, home, sweet, sweet, home!
There's no place like home, oh, there's no place like
home!

John Howard Payne

Ring out, wild bells

Ring out, wild bells, to the wild sky,
The flying cloud, the frosty light:
The year is dying in the night;
Ring out, wild bells, and let him die.

Ring out the old, ring in the new,
Ring, happy bells, across the snow:
The year is going, let him go;
Ring out the false, ring in the true.

Ring out the grief that saps the mind
For those that here we see no more;
Ring out the feud of rich and poor,
Ring in redress to all mankind.

Ring out a slowly dying cause,
And ancient forms of party strife;
Ring in the nobler modes of life,
With sweeter manners, purer laws.

Ring out the want, the care, the sin,
The faithless coldness of the times;
Ring out, ring out my mournful rhymes
But ring the fuller minstrel in.

Ring out false pride in place and blood,
The civic slander and the spite;
Ring in the love of truth and right,
Ring in the common love of good.

Ring out old shapes of foul disease;
Ring out the narrowing lust of gold;
Ring out the thousand wars of old,
Ring in the thousand years of peace.

Ring in the valiant man and free,
The larger heart, the kindlier hand;
Ring out the darkness of the land,
Ring in the Christ that is to be.

Alfred Lord Tennyson

Christmas Greetings

Lady dear, if Fairies may
For a moment lay aside
Cunning tricks and elfish play,
'Tis at happy Christmas-tide.

We have heard the children say -
Gentle children, whom we love -
Long ago, on Christmas Day,
Came a message from above.

Still, as Christmas-tide comes round,
They remember it again -
Echo still the joyful sound
'Peace on earth, good-will to men!'

Yet the hearts must childlike be
Where such heavenly guests abide:
Unto children, in their glee,
All the year is Christmas-tide!

Thus, forgetting tricks and play
For a moment, Lady dear,
We would wish you, if we may,
Merry Christmas, glad New Year!

Lewis Carroll

Christmas in India

Dim dawn behind the tamarisks—the sky is
saffron-yellow—
As the women in the village grind the corn,
And the parrots seek the riverside, each calling to
his fellow
That the Day, the staring Eastern Day, is born.
Oh the white dust on the highway! Oh the stenches
in the byway!
Oh the clammy fog that hovers over earth!
And at Home they're making merry 'neath the white
and scarlet berry—
What part have India's exiles in their mirth?

Full day behind the tamarisks—the sky is blue and
staring—
As the cattle crawl afield beneath the yoke,
And they bear One o'er the field-path, who is past
all hope or caring,
To the ghat below the curling wreaths of smoke.
Call on Rama, going slowly, as ye bear a brother

lowly—
Call on Rama—he may hear, perhaps, your voice!
With our hymn-books and our psalters we appeal to
other altars,
And to-day we bid "good Christian men rejoice!"

High noon behind the tamarisks—the sun is hot
above us—
As at Home the Christmas Day is breaking wan.
They will drink our healths at dinner—those who
tell us how they love us,
And forget us till another year be gone!
Oh the toil that knows no breaking! Oh the
Heimweh, ceaseless, aching!
Oh the black dividing Sea and alien Plain!
Youth was cheap—wherefore we sold it. Gold was
good—we hoped to hold it,
And to-day we know the fulness of our gain.

Grey dusk behind the tamarisks—the parrots fly
together—
As the sun is sinking slowly over Home;
And his last ray seems to mock us shackled in a
lifelong tether.
That drags us back how'er so far we roam.
Hard her service, poor her payment—she in ancient,
tattered raiment—
India, she the grim Stepmother of our kind.

If a year of life be lent her, if her temple's shrine we
enter,
The door is shut—we may not look behind.

Black night behind the tamarisks—the owls begin
their chorus —
As the conches from the temple scream and bray.
With the fruitless years behind us, and the hopeless
years before us,
Let us honour, O my brother, Christmas Day!
Call a truce, then, to our labours—let us feast with
friends and neighbours,
And be merry as the custom of our caste;
For if "faint and forced the laughter," and if sadness
follow after,
We are richer by one mocking Christmas past.

Rudyard Kipling

The Three Kings

Three Kings came riding from far away,
  Melchior and Gaspar and Baltasar;
Three Wise Men out of the East were they,
And they travelled by night and they slept by day,
  For their guide was a beautiful, wonderful star.

The star was so beautiful, large and clear,
  That all the other stars of the sky
Became a white mist in the atmosphere,
And by this they knew that the coming was near
  Of the Prince foretold in the prophecy.

Three caskets they bore on their saddle-bows,
  Three caskets of gold with golden keys;
Their robes were of crimson silk with rows
Of bells and pomegranates and furbelows,
  Their turbans like blossoming almond-trees.

And so the Three Kings rode into the West,
Through the dusk of the night, over hill and dell,

And sometimes they nodded with beard on breast,
And sometimes talked, as they paused to rest,
With the people they met at some wayside well.

"Of the child that is born," said Baltasar,
"Good people, I pray you, tell us the news;
For we in the East have seen his star,
And have ridden fast, and have ridden far,
To find and worship the King of the Jews."

And the people answered, "You ask in vain;
We know of no King but Herod the Great!"
They thought the Wise Men were men insane,
As they spurred their horses across the plain,
Like riders in haste, who cannot wait.

And when they came to Jerusalem,
Herod the Great, who had heard this thing,
Sent for the Wise Men and questioned them;
And said, "Go down unto Bethlehem,
And bring me tidings of this new king."

So they rode away; and the star stood still,
The only one in the grey of morn;
Yes, it stopped—it stood still of its own free will,
Right over Bethlehem on the hill,
The city of David, where Christ was born.

And the Three Kings rode through the gate and the
guard,
Through the silent street, till their horses turned
And neighed as they entered the great inn-yard;
But the windows were closed, and the doors were
barred,
And only a light in the stable burned.

And cradled there in the scented hay,
In the air made sweet by the breath of kine,
The little child in the manger lay,
The child, that would be king one day
Of a kingdom not human, but divine.

His mother Mary of Nazareth
Sat watching beside his place of rest,
Watching the even flow of his breath,
For the joy of life and the terror of death
Were mingled together in her breast.

They laid their offerings at his feet:
The gold was their tribute to a King,
The frankincense, with its odor sweet,
Was for the Priest, the Paraclete,
The myrrh for the body's burying.

And the mother wondered and bowed her head,
And sat as still as a statue of stone,

Her heart was troubled yet comforted,
Remembering what the Angel had said
Of an endless reign and of David's throne.

Then the Kings rode out of the city gate,
With a clatter of hoofs in proud array;
But they went not back to Herod the Great,
For they knew his malice and feared his hate,
And returned to their homes by another way.

Henry Wadsworth Longfellow

Christmas at Sea

The sheets were frozen hard, and they cut the naked
hand;
The decks were like a slide, where a seaman scarce
could stand;
The wind was a nor'wester, blowing squally off the
sea;
And cliffs and spouting breakers were the only
things a-lee.

They heard the surf a-roaring before the break of
day;
But 'twas only with the peep of light we saw how ill
we lay.
We tumbled every hand on deck instanter, with a
shout,
And we gave her the maintops'l, and stood by to go
about.

All day we tacked and tacked between the South
Head and the North;

All day we hauled the frozen sheets, and got no
further forth;
All day as cold as charity, in bitter pain and dread,
For very life and nature we tacked from head to
head.

We gave the South a wider berth, for there the
tide-race roared;
But every tack we made we brought the North Head
close aboard:
So's we saw the cliffs and houses, and the breakers
running high,
And the coastguard in his garden, with his glass
against his eye.

The frost was on the village roofs as white as ocean
foam;
The good red fires were burning bright in every
'long-shore home;
The windows sparkled clear, and the chimneys
volleyed out;
And I vow we sniffed the victuals as the vessel went
about.

The bells upon the church were rung with a mighty
jovial cheer;
For it's just that I should tell you how (of all days in
the year)

This day of our adversity was blessed Christmas
morn,
And the house above the coastguard's was the house
where I was born.

O well I saw the pleasant room, the pleasant faces
there,
My mother's silver spectacles, my father's silver
hair;
And well I saw the firelight, like a flight of homely
elves,
Go dancing round the china-plates that stand upon
the shelves.

And well I knew the talk they had, the talk that was
of me,
Of the shadow on the household and the son that
went to sea;
And O the wicked fool I seemed, in every kind of way,
To be here and hauling frozen ropes on blessed
Christmas Day.

They lit the high sea-light, and the dark began to
fall.
"All hands to loose topgallant sails," I heard the
captain call.
"By the Lord, she'll never stand it," our first mate
Jackson, cried.

55

..."It's the one way or the other, Mr. Jackson," he
replied.

She staggered to her bearings, but the sails were
new and good,
And the ship smelt up to windward just as though
she understood.
As the winter's day was ending, in the entry of the
night,
We cleared the weary headland, and passed below
the light.

And they heaved a mighty breath, every soul on
board but me,
As they saw her nose again pointing handsome out
to sea;
But all that I could think of, in the darkness and the
cold,
Was just that I was leaving home and my folks were
growing old.

Robert Louis Stevenson

The Snowflake

Before I melt,
Come, look at me!
This lovely icy filigree!
Of a great forest
In one night
I make a wilderness
Of white:
By skyey cold
Of crystals made,
All softly, on
Your finger laid,
I pause, that you
My beauty see:
Breathe; and I vanish
Instantly.

Walter de la Mare

Before the Ice is in the Pools

Before the ice is in the pools—
Before the skaters go,
Or any check at nightfall
Is tarnished by the snow—

Before the fields have finished,
Before the Christmas tree,
Wonder upon wonder
Will arrive to me!

Emily Dickinson

A Carol From Flanders

In Flanders on the Christmas morn
The trenched foemen lay,
the German and the Briton born,
And it was Christmas Day.

The red sun rose on fields accurst,
The gray fog fled away;
But neither cared to fire the first,
For it was Christmas Day!

They called from each to each across
The hideous disarray,
For terrible has been their loss:
"Oh, this is Christmas Day!"

Their rifles all they set aside,
One impulse to obey;
'Twas just the men on either side,
Just men — and Christmas Day.

Frederick Niven

Christmas in the Heart

The snow lies deep upon the ground,
And winter's brightness all around
Decks bravely out the forest sere,
With jewels of the brave old year.
The coasting crowd upon the hill
With some new spirit seems to thrill;
And all the temple bells achime.
Ring out the glee of Christmas time.

In happy homes the brown oak-bough
Vies with the red-gemmed holly now;
And here and there, like pearls, there show
The berries of the mistletoe.
A sprig upon the chandelier
Says to the maidens, "Come not here!"
Even the pauper of the earth
Some kindly gift has cheered to mirth!

Within his chamber, dim and cold,
There sits a grasping miser old.

He has no thought save one of gain, —
To grind and gather and grasp and drain.
A peal of bells, a merry shout
Assail his ear: he gazes out
Upon a world to him all gray,
And snarls, "Why, this is Christmas Day!"

No, man of ice, — for shame, for shame!
For "Christmas Day" is no mere name.
No, not for you this ringing cheer,
This festal season of the year.
And not for you the chime of bells
From holy temple rolls and swells.
In day and deed he has no part—
Who holds not Christmas in his heart!

Paul Laurence Dunbar

When Icicles Hang by the Wall

When icicles hang by the wall,
And Dick the shepherd blows his nail,
And Tom bears logs into the hall,
And milk comes frozen home in pail,
When blood is nipp'd, and ways be foul,
Then nightly sings the staring owl:
'Tu-who;
Tu-whit, Tu-who' – A merry note,
While greasy Joan doth keel the pot.

When all aloud the wind doth blow,
And coughing drowns the parson's saw,
And birds sit brooding in the snow,
And Marian's nose looks red and raw,
When roasted crabs hiss in the bowl,
Then nightly sings the staring owl:
'Tu-who;
Tu-whit, Tu-who' – A merry note,
While greasy Joan doth keel the pot.

William Shakespeare

A Christmas Ghost Story

South of the Line, inland from far Durban,
A mouldering soldier lies—your countryman.
Awry and doubled up are his gray bones,
And on the breeze his puzzled phantom moans
Nightly to clear Canopus: "I would know
By whom and when the All-Earth-gladdening Law
Of Peace, brought in by that Man Crucified,
Was ruled to be inept, and set aside?
And what of logic or of truth appears
In tacking 'Anno Domini' to the years?
Near twenty-hundred livened thus have hied,
But tarries yet the Cause for which He died."

Thomas Hardy

The Waiting

I wait and watch: before my eyes
Methinks the night grows thin and gray;
I wait and watch the eastern skies
To see the golden spears uprise
Beneath the oriflamme of day!

Like one whose limbs are bound in trance
I hear the day-sounds swell and grow,
And see across the twilight glance,
Troop after troop, in swift advance,
The shining ones with plumes of snow!

I know the errand of their feet,
I know what mighty work is theirs;
I can but lift up hands unmeet,
The threshing-floors of God to beat,
And speed them with unworthy prayers.

I will not dream in vain despair
The steps of progress wait for me

The puny leverage of a hair
The planet's impulse well may spare,
    A drop of dew the tided sea.

The loss, if loss there be, is mine,
    And yet not mine if understood;
For one shall grasp and one resign,
One drink life's rue, and one its wine,
And God shall make the balance good.

Oh power to do! Oh baffled will!
Oh prayer and action! ye are one.
Who may not strive, may yet fulfil
The harder task of standing still,
And good but wished with God is done!

John Greenleaf Whittier

The First Snowfall

The snow had begun in the gloaming,
And busily all the night
Had been heaping field and highway
With a silence deep and white.

Every pine and fir and hemlock
Wore ermine too dear for an earl,
And the poorest twig on the elm-tree
Was ridged inch deep with pearl.

From sheds new-roofed with Carrara
Came Chanticleer's muffled crow,
The stiff rails were softened to swan's-down,
And still fluttered down the snow.

I stood and watched by the window
The noiseless work of the sky,
And the sudden flurries of snow-birds,
Like brown leaves whirling by.

I thought of a mound in sweet Auburn
Where a little headstone stood;
How the flakes were folding it gently,
As did robins the babes in the wood.

Up spoke our own little Mabel,
Saying, 'Father, who makes it snow?'
And I told of the good All-father
Who cares for us here below.

Again I looked at the snowfall,
And thought of the leaden sky
That arched o'er our first great sorrow,
When that mound was heaped so high.

I remembered the gradual patience
That fell from that cloud like snow,
Flake by flake, healing and hiding
The scar that renewed our woe.

And again to the child I whispered,
'The snow that husheth all,
Darling, the merciful Father
Alone can make it fall!'

Then, with eyes that saw not, I kissed her;
And she, kissing back, could not know
That my kiss was given to her sister,

Folded close under deepening snow

James Russell Lowell

Sheep in Winter

The sheep get up and make their many tracks
And bear a load of snow upon their backs,
And gnaw the frozen turnip to the ground
With sharp quick bite, and then go noising round
The boy that pecks the turnips all the day
And knocks his hands to keep the cold away
And laps his legs in straw to keep them warm
And hides behind the hedges from the storm.
The sheep, as tame as dogs, go where he goes
And try to shake their fleeces from the snows,
Then leave their frozen meal and wander round
The stubble stack that stands beside the ground,
And lie all night and face the drizzling storm
And shun the hovel where they might be warm.

‘

John Clare

Old Santeclaus

Old Santeclaus with much delight
His reindeer drives this frosty night,
O'er chimney-tops, and tracks of snow,
To bring his yearly gifts to you.

The steady friend of virtuous youth,
The friend of duty, and of truth,
Each Christmas eve he joys to come
Where love and peace have made their home.

Through many houses he has been,
And various beds and stockings seen;
Some, white as snow, and neatly mended,
Others, that seemed for pigs intended.

Where e'er I found good girls or boys,
That hated quarrels, strife and noise,
I left an apple, or a tart,
Or wooden gun, or painted cart.

To some I gave a pretty doll,
To some a peg-top, or a ball;
No crackers, cannons, squibs, or rockets,
To blow their eyes up, or their pockets.

No drums to stun their Mother's ear,
Nor swords to make their sisters fear;
But pretty books to store their mind
With knowledge of each various kind.

But where I found the children naughty,
In manners rude, in temper haughty,
Thankless to parents, liars, swearers,
Boxers, or cheats, or base tale-bearers,

I left a long, black, birchen rod,
Such as the dread command of God
Directs a Parent's hand to use
When virtue's path his sons refuse.

Clement Clarke Moore

Christmas Trees

The city had withdrawn into itself
And left at last the country to the country;
When between whirls of snow not come to lie
And whirls of foliage not yet laid, there drove
A stranger to our yard, who looked the city,
Yet did in country fashion in that there
He sat and waited till he drew us out
A-buttoning coats to ask him who he was.
He proved to be the city come again
To look for something it had left behind
And could not do without and keep its Christmas.
He asked if I would sell my Christmas trees;
My woods—the young fir balsams like a place
Where houses all are churches and have spires.
I hadn't thought of them as Christmas Trees.
I doubt if I was tempted for a moment
To sell them off their feet to go in cars
And leave the slope behind the house all bare,
Where the sun shines now no warmer than the
moon.

I'd hate to have them know it if I was.
Yet more I'd hate to hold my trees except
As others hold theirs or refuse for them,
Beyond the time of profitable growth,
The trial by market everything must come to.
I dallied so much with the thought of selling.
Then whether from mistaken courtesy
And fear of seeming short of speech, or whether
From hope of hearing good of what was mine, I said,
"There aren't enough to be worth while."
"I could soon tell how many they would cut,
You let me look them over."

"You could look.
But don't expect I'm going to let you have them."
Pasture they spring in, some in clumps too close
That lop each other of boughs, but not a few
Quite solitary and having equal boughs
All round and round. The latter he nodded "Yes" to,
Or paused to say beneath some lovelier one,
With a buyer's moderation, "That would do."
I thought so too, but wasn't there to say so.
We climbed the pasture on the south, crossed over,
And came down on the north. He said, "A
thousand."

"A thousand Christmas trees!—at what apiece?"

He felt some need of softening that to me:
"A thousand trees would come to thirty dollars."

Then I was certain I had never meant
To let him have them. Never show surprise!
But thirty dollars seemed so small beside
The extent of pasture I should strip, three cents
(For that was all they figured out apiece),
Three cents so small beside the dollar friends
I should be writing to within the hour
Would pay in cities for good trees like those,
Regular vestry-trees whole Sunday Schools
Could hang enough on to pick off enough.
A thousand Christmas trees I didn't know I had!
Worth three cents more to give away than sell,
As may be shown by a simple calculation.
Too bad I couldn't lay one in a letter.
I can't help wishing I could send you one,
In wishing you herewith a Merry Christmas.

Robert Frost

By The Hearth-Stone

By the hearth-stone
She sits alone,
The long night bearing:
With eyes that gleam
Into the dream
Of the firelight staring.

Low and more low
The dying glow
Burns in the embers;
She nothing heeds
And nothing needs — -
Only remembers.

Sir Henry Newbolt

The Burning Babe

As I in hoary winter's night stood shivering in the
snow,
Surprised I was with sudden heat which made my
heart to glow;
And lifting up a fearful eye to view what fire was
near,
A pretty babe all burning bright did in the air appear;
Who, though scorched with excessive heat, such
floods of tears did shed,
As though his floods should quench his flames,
which with his tears were fed.
"Alas," quoth he, "but newly born, in fiery heats I
fry,
Yet none approach to warm their hearts, or feel my
fire but I!
My faultless breast the furnace is, the fuel wounding
thorns,
Love is the fire, and sighs the smoke, the ashes
shame and scorns;
The fuel justice layeth on, and mercy blows the

coals,
The metal in this furnace wrought are men's defiled souls,
For which, as now on fire I am to work them to their good,
So will I melt into a bath to wash them in my blood."
With this he vanished out of sight and swiftly shrunk away,
And straight I called unto mind that it was Christmas Day.

Robert Southwell

A Song for New Year's Eve

Stay yet, my friends, a moment stay—
     Stay till the good old year,
So long companion of our way,
     Shakes hands, and leaves us here.
          Oh stay, oh stay,
     One little hour, and then away.

The year, whose hopes were high and strong,
     Has now no hopes to wake;
Yet one hour more of jest and song
     For his familiar sake.
          Oh stay, oh stay,
     One mirthful hour, and then away.

The kindly year, his liberal hands
     Have lavished all his store.
And shall we turn from where he stands,
     Because he gives no more?
          Oh stay, oh stay,
     One grateful hour, and then away.

Days brightly came and calmly went,
While yet he was our guest;
How cheerfully the week was spent!
How sweet the seventh day's rest!
Oh stay, oh stay,
One golden hour, and then away.

Dear friends were with us, some who sleep
Beneath the coffin-lid:
What pleasant memories we keep
Of all they said and did!
Oh stay, oh stay,
One tender hour, and then away.

Even while we sing, he smiles his last,
And leaves our sphere behind.
The good old year is with the past;
Oh be the new as kind!
Oh stay, oh stay,
One parting strain, and then away.

William Cullen Bryant

The Walrus And The Carpenter

The sun was shining on the sea,
    Shining with all his might:
He did his very best to make
    The billows smooth and bright—
And this was odd, because it was
    The middle of the night.

The moon was shining sulkily,
    Because she thought the sun
Had got no business to be there
    After the day was done—
"It's very rude of him," she said,
    "To come and spoil the fun!"

The sea was wet as wet could be,
    The sands were dry as dry.
You could not see a cloud, because
    No cloud was in the sky:
No birds were flying overhead—
    There were no birds to fly.

The Walrus and the Carpenter
Were walking close at hand;
They wept like anything to see
Such quantities of sand:
"If this were only cleared away,"
They said, "it would be grand!"

"If seven maids with seven mops
Swept it for half a year.
Do you suppose," the Walrus said,
"That they could get it clear?"
"I doubt it," said the Carpenter,
And shed a bitter tear.

"O Oysters, come and walk with us!"
The Walrus did beseech.
"A pleasant walk, a pleasant talk,
Along the briny beach:
We cannot do with more than four,
To give a hand to each."

The eldest Oyster looked at him,
But never a word he said:
The eldest Oyster winked his eye,
And shook his heavy head—
Meaning to say he did not choose
To leave the oyster-bed.

But four young Oysters hurried up,
All eager for the treat:
Their coats were brushed, their faces washed,
Their shoes were clean and neat—
And this was odd, because, you know,
They hadn't any feet.

Four other Oysters followed them,
And yet another four;
And thick and fast they came at last,
And more, and more, and more—
All hopping through the frothy waves,
And scrambling to the shore.

The Walrus and the Carpenter
Walked on a mile or so,
And then they rested on a rock
Conveniently low:
And all the little Oysters stood
And waited in a row.

"The time has come," the Walrus said,
"To talk of many things:
Of shoes—and ships—and sealing-wax—
Of cabbages—and kings—
And why the sea is boiling hot—
And whether pigs have wings."

"But wait a bit," the Oysters cried,
  "Before we have our chat;
For some of us are out of breath,
  And all of us are fat!"
"No hurry!" said the Carpenter.
  They thanked him much for that.

"A loaf of bread," the Walrus said,
  "Is what we chiefly need:
Pepper and vinegar besides
  Are very good indeed—
Now if you're ready, Oysters dear,
  We can begin to feed."

"But not on us!" the Oysters cried,
  Turning a little blue.
"After such kindness, that would be
  A dismal thing to do!"
"The night is fine," the Walrus said.
  "Do you admire the view?

"It was so kind of you to come!
  And you are very nice!"
The Carpenter said nothing but
  "Cut us another slice:
I wish you were not quite so deaf—
  I've had to ask you twice!"

"It seems a shame," the Walrus said,
"To play them such a trick,
After we've brought them out so far,
And made them trot so quick!"
The Carpenter said nothing but
"The butter's spread too thick!"

"I weep for you," the Walrus said:
"I deeply sympathize."
With sobs and tears he sorted out
Those of the largest size,
Holding his pocket-handkerchief
Before his streaming eyes.

"O Oysters," said the Carpenter,
"You've had a pleasant run!
Shall we be trotting home again?'
But answer came there none—
And this was scarcely odd, because
They'd eaten every one.

Lewis Carroll

The Lamb

Little lamb, who made thee?
Dost thou know who made thee,
Gave thee life, and bid thee feed
By the stream and o'er the mead;
Gave thee clothing of delight,
Softest clothing, woolly, bright;
Gave thee such a tender voice,
Making all the vales rejoice?
Little lamb, who made thee?
Dost thou know who made thee?

Little lamb, I'll tell thee;
Little lamb, I'll tell thee:
He is called by thy name,
For He calls Himself a Lamb.
He is meek, and He is mild,
He became a little child.
I a child, and thou a lamb,
We are called by His name.
Little lamb, God bless thee!

Little lamb, God bless thee!

William Blake

New Prince, New Pomp

Behold a silly tender Babe, in freezing winter night;
In homely manger trembling lies, alas a piteous
sight:
The inns are full, no man will yield this little Pilgrim
bed,
But forced He is with silly beasts, in crib to shroud
His head.
Despise Him not for lying there, first what He is
enquire:
An orient pearl is often found, in depth of dirty mire;
Weigh not His crib, His wooden dish, nor beasts that
by Him feed:
Weigh not His mother's poor attire, nor Joseph's
simple weed.
This stable is a Prince's court, the crib His chair of
state:
The beasts are parcel of His pomp, the wooden dish
His plate.
The persons in that poor attire, His royal liveries
wear,

The Prince Himself is come from heaven, this pomp
is prized there.
With joy approach, O Christian wight, do homage to
thy King,
And highly prize this humble pomp, which He from
heaven doth bring.

Robert Southwell

The New-year's Gift

Let others look for pearl and gold,
Tissues, or tabbies manifold:
One only lock of that sweet hay
Whereon the blessed Baby lay,
Or one poor swaddling-clout, shall be
The richest New-year's gift to me.

Robert Herrick

A Hymn on the Nativity of My Savior

I sing the birth was born tonight,
The Author both of life and light;
The angels so did sound it,
And like the ravished shepherds said,
Who saw the light, and were afraid,
Yet searched, and true they found it.

The Son of God, the eternal King,
That did us all salvation bring,
And freed the soul from danger;
He whom the whole world could not take,
The Word, which heaven and earth did make,
Was now laid in a manger.

The Father's wisdom willed it so,
The Son's obedience knew no "No,"
Both wills were in one stature;
And as that wisdom had decreed,
The Word was now made Flesh indeed,
And took on Him our nature.

What comfort by Him do we win?
Who made Himself the Prince of sin,
To make us heirs of glory?
To see this Babe, all innocence,
A Martyr born in our defense,
Can man forget this story?

Ben Jonson

Author's Note

Christmas has never really been my thing – the grey drizzle of Manchester usually made it more of a damp affair than a sparkling winter wonderland. But, there's something about the quiet moments, spent with family, that brings warmth to an otherwise cold season. And that's what I've always found special about festive poetry.

The poems in this collection capture that sense of warmth in different ways. Whether it's the nostalgia of childhood Christmases, the simple beauty of winter landscapes, or the joy found in familiar traditions, these verses offer a break from the noise and commercialism of the holiday. Some poems are light-hearted and joyful, others reflect on the season's quieter, more reflective side. Together, they paint a fuller picture of what the festive season can be – beyond the tinsel and bright lights.

As someone who looks forward more to Boxing Day

football than Christmas morning, these poems give a different kind of comfort. They remind me that the season isn't just about what you see on the outside, but about the connections we make and the moments we share, even when the sky's grey.

I hope you find something in this collection that resonates with you, whether you're all about Christmas or just enjoy a good poem by the fire.

Printed in Great Britain
by Amazon

53823332R00057